Writing a Cryptosystem Encoding RSA Code in C Language

Alexios Iosif Kotsis

Bibliographic information published by the German National Library:

The German National Library lists this publication in the National Bibliography; detailed bibliographic data are available on the Internet at http://dnb.dnb.de.

ISBN: 9783346104953
This book is also available as an ebook.

© GRIN Publishing GmbH
Trappentreustraße 1
80339 München

Print and binding: Books on Demand GmbH, Norderstedt, Germany
Printed on acid-free paper from responsible sources.

The present work has been carefully prepared. Nevertheless, authors and publishers do not incur liability for the correctness of information, notes, links and advice as well as any printing errors.

GRIN web shop: https://www.grin.com/document/512169

Alexios Iosif Kotsis

Cryptosystem encrypting RSA Code Programming

Table of Contents

1. Objectives

The purpose of this paper is to write a cryptosystem encoding RSA code in C language and verify it mathematically.

RSA is one of the first public-key cryptosystems and is widely used for secure data transmission. In such a cryptosystem, the encryption key is public, and it is different from the decryption key which is kept secret.

2. Components

Laptop with *Linux running*

3. Design - Procedure

Choose two prime numbers p and q (these are your inputs). Suppose that you need to send a message to your friend, and you implement the RSA algorithm for secure key generation. You need public and private keys (these are your outputs). You are free to choose other parameters or inputs if you need any. Write a program for the RSA algorithm using any programing language such as C to generate your public and private key.

Your program will display the following:
  (1) public and private keys
  (2) your given message and encrypted message
  (3) a message for any wrong inputs such as "you entered a number, which is not a prime."

To do that we used the following code:

```
File  Edit  View  Search  Terminal  Help
#include <stdio.h>
#include <stdlib.h>
#include <string.h>
#include <math.h>
#include <ctype.h>

long int p,q,t=0,n,m,d,pp,pp2,P,C,flag=0;

int a,b,i,j;
int count;

double em,en,en2;
double ez,ez2=5.0;
int  i2=1;



int gcd(int a)
{
// Finds the GCD and then asks the user to pick one of the related prime numbers between 1<e<m

        int remainder = 2;
        int divident,divisor;

//      printf("Enter Number\n");
//       scanf("%d",&p);

        for(i = 2 ; i < a ; i++){

                divident = a;
                divisor = i;

                while(divisor != 0){

                        remainder = divident % divisor;
                        divident  = divisor;
                        divisor   = remainder;
                }

                if(divident  == 1){
                        printf("Relatively Prime Number is : %d \n" ,i);
                }
        }
        printf("\nChoose a number\n");
        scanf("%d", &pp);
        return pp;
}
```

4

```c
double de(int m, int pp2)
{
        //Function de will do the operation ((i2*m)+1)/e
        //i2 is the counter number
        //If the operation has any remainders, it will loop back

        em = (i2*m)+1;
//      printf("\nw %f\n",em);
        en2 = em;
        en = em/pp2;
//      printf("\nwo %f\n",en);
        ez = fmod(em,pp2);
//      printf("\nwo2 %f\n",ez);

        if(ez!=0){
                i2++;
                return de(m,pp2);
        }

        return en;
}

int EncryKey(int count, int n){

        int startP,x=0,Cnew;
        printf("\nChoose a value for P: ");
        scanf("%d",&startP);
//      printf("%d", startP);

        x = pow(startP, count);
        Cnew = x%n;
//      printf("\n%d\n",Cnew);

        return Cnew;

}

int DecryKey(int C, int d, int n){

        int Pnew, x=0;

        x = pow(C, d);
//      printf("\n%d\n",x);
        Pnew = x%n;
//      printf("\n%d\n",Pnew);

        return Pnew;
```

```c
}
int main()
{
//    clrscr();
      printf("\nEnter the first prime number: ");
      scanf("%d",&p);
      t=p/2;
      for(i=2;i<=t;i++){
            if(p%i==0){
                  printf("\nYou entered a number which is not a prime\n"); //If it's not a prime it will loop back to main and ask again
//                getch();
                  return main();
            }
      }

      m=0;
      printf("\nEnter the second prime number: ");
      scanf("%d",&q);
      t=q/2;
      for(i=2;i<=t;i++){
            if(q%i==0){
                  printf("\nYou enterered a number which is not prime\n"); //If it's not a prime it will loop back to main and ask again
                  return main();
            }
      }
      n = p*q;
      m = (p-1)*(q-1);
//    printf("%d\n",m);
      count = gcd(m);
      d = de(m,count);
      C = EncryKey(count, n);
      P = DecryKey(C, d, n);
      printf("\nThe public key is {%d, %d}\n", count, n); //The following will print the private, public keys and the encrypted message
      printf("\nThe private key is {%d, %d}\n", d, n);
      printf("\nThe encypted message is: %d\n",C);
      printf("\nThe decrypted message is: %d\n",P);
      return 0;
```

6

To verify the proper working of the code and the results we used mathematical calculations.

4. RSA - Mathematical

Steps of RSA implementation:

1. Select two prime numbers, **p = 3** and **q = 11**

2. Calculate **n = pq = 3 x 11 = 33**

3. Calculate **m = (3- 1) (11 - 1) = 2 x 10 = 20**

4. Select **e** such that **e** is relatively prime to **m = 20** and less than **m, 1 < e < 20**

gcd (e, 20) = 1

20 = 1 x 2 x 10

    = 1 x 2 x 2 x 5

    = 1 x 2^2 x 5

Assume that we take the smallest prime number in between of 2, 5 to 20, so **e = 3**

You also can take other value as long as it fulfils the conditions – it must be relatively prime with 20 and it is less than 20

. Determine **d** such that **de = 1 mod 20** and **d < 20**

de mod **m = 1**

d x 3 = (? X 20) + 1

1 x 20 + 1 = 20 + 1 = 21	**21/3 = 7**
2 x 20 + 1 = 40 + 1 = 41	41/3 = 13.6

Find the value which when the results mod 3 with no remainder

The correct value is **d = 7**, because

7 x 3 = 21 = 1 x 20 + 1

You also can take other value as long as it is a positive integer

Therefore, n = 33, m = 20, e = 3, d = 7

The resulting keys are:

Public key = {e, n} and Private key = {d, n}

Public key = {3, 33} and Private key = {7, 33}

Assume that **P** is the plaintext and **C** is the ciphertext

The encryption is $C = P^3 \bmod 33$

The decryption is $P = C^7 \bmod 33$

Public key = {e, n} and Private key = {d, n}

Public key = {3, 33} and Private key = {7, 33}

Given **P = 6**

The encryption is $C = P^3 \bmod 33$

7

$C = 6^3 \bmod 33$

$= 216 \bmod 33$

$= 18$

The decryption is $P = C^7 \bmod 33$

$P = 18^7 \bmod 33$

$= 6$

We then input the same numbers as the example and check the result produced by the code.

We first inserted number 8 which is not a prime number and the program responded correctly that it is not a prime number.

The prime input numbers inserted, according to the example, were 3 and 11 and then e was chosen as e=3. Then P=6 to be encrypted was chosen. The results and calculations were as follows in the next picture **with public key {3,13} and Private key (7,13}** The code produced **a correct encrypted message for P as 18 and correct decrypted message as 6,** verifying example 3.

```
File   Edit   View   Search   Terminal   Help
root@kali:~/Desktop/5650#  ./LabAssignment11

Enter the first prime number: 8

You entered a number which is not a prime

Enter the first prime number: 3

Enter the second prime number: 11
Relatively Prime Number is : 3
Relatively Prime Number is : 7
Relatively Prime Number is : 9
Relatively Prime Number is : 11
Relatively Prime Number is : 13
Relatively Prime Number is : 17
Relatively Prime Number is : 19

Choose a number
3

Choose a value for P: 6

The public key is {3, 33}

The private key is {7, 33}

The encypted message is: 18

The decrypted message is: 6
root@kali:~/Desktop/5650#
```

The code in text, according to the instructions, is as follows:

```c
#include <stdio.h>
#include <stdlib.h>
#include <string.h>
#include <math.h>
#include <ctype.h>

long int p,q,t=0,n,m,d,pp,pp2,P,C,flag=0;

int a,b,i,j;
int count;

double em,en,en2;
double ez,ez2=5.0;
 int  i2=1;

 int gcd(int a)
 {
// Finds the GCD and then asks the user to pick one of the related prime   numbers
between 1<e<m

 int remainder = 2;
 int divident,divisor;

//     printf("Enter Number\n");
//      scanf("%d",&p);

 for(i = 2 ; i < a ; i++){

 divident  = a;
 divisor = i;

 while(divisor != 0){

 remainder = divident % divisor;
 divident  = divisor;
```

```c
    divisor  = remainder;
        }

    if(divident  == 1){
    printf("Relatively Prime Number is : %d \n" ,i);
        }
}
printf("\nChoose a number\n");
scanf("%d", &pp);
return pp;
}


double de(int m, int pp2)

{

//Function de will do the operation ((i2*m)+1)/e
//i2 is the counter number
//If the operation has any remainders, it will loop back

em = (i2*m)+1;
//    printf("\nw %f\n",em);
en2 = em;
en = em/pp2;
//    printf("\nwo %f\n",en);
ez = fmod(em,pp2);
//    printf("\nwo2 %f\n",ez);

if(ez!=0){
i2++;
return de(m,pp2);
}

return en;
}

int EncryKey(int count, int n){
int startP,x=0,Cnew;
```

```c
    printf("\nChoose a value for P: ");
    scanf("%d",&startP);
//  printf("%d", startP);

    x = pow(startP, count);
    Cnew = x%n;
//  printf("\n%d\n",Cnew);

    return Cnew;

}

    int DecryKey(int C, int d, int n){

    int Pnew, x=0;

    x = pow(C, d);
//  printf("\n%d\n",x);
    Pnew = x%n;
//  printf("\n%d\n",Pnew);

    return Pnew;

    }
Int main()
    {
//  clrscr();
    printf("\nEnter the first prime number: ");
    scanf("%d",&p);
    t=p/2;
    for(i=2;i<=t;i++){
    if(p%i==0){
    printf("\nYou entered a number which is not a prime\n"); //If it's not a prime it
will loop back to main and ask again
//  getch():
    return main();
```
11

```
          }
      }

      m=0;
      printf("\nEnter the second prime number: ");
      scanf("%d",&q);
      t=q/2;
      for(i=2;i<=t;i++){
      if(q%i==0){
      printf("\nYou enterered a number which is not prime\n"); //If it's not a prime it will
loop back to main and ask again
      return main();
          }
      }
      n = p*q;
      m = (p-1)*(q-1);
//    printf("%d\n",m);
      count = gcd(m);
      d = de(m,count);
      C = EncryKey(count, n);
      P = DecryKey(C, d, n);
      printf("\nThe public key is {%d, %d}\n", count, n); //The following will print the
private, public keys and the encrypted message
      printf("\nThe private key is {%d, %d}\n", d, n);
      printf("\nThe encypted message is: %d\n",C);
      printf("\nThe decrypted message is: %d\n",P);
      return 0;
}
```

5. Conclusions

The RSA code was created correctly using C language and proven accordingly with the numerical
example.